Calligraphy Practice Book

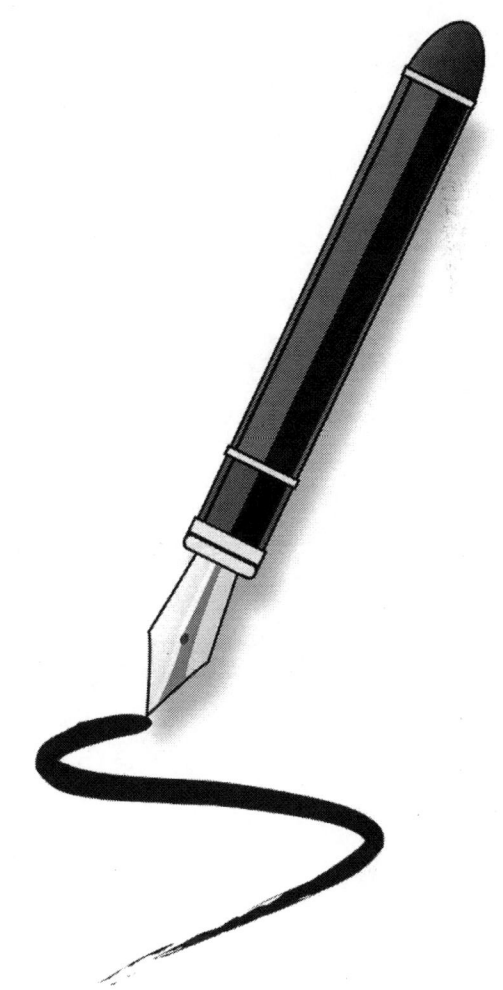

Creative Calligraphy & Hand Lettering Notebook Paper

Copyright 2017 Blank Books 'N' Juornals
All Rights Reserved. This book or any part of it may not be used
in any matter whatsoever without the expressed written permission
of the publisher except for the use of brief quotations in a book review

What's Inside This Book

4 Styles of Calligraphy Practice Paper

Feint Lines With Over 100 Pages

Paper 1

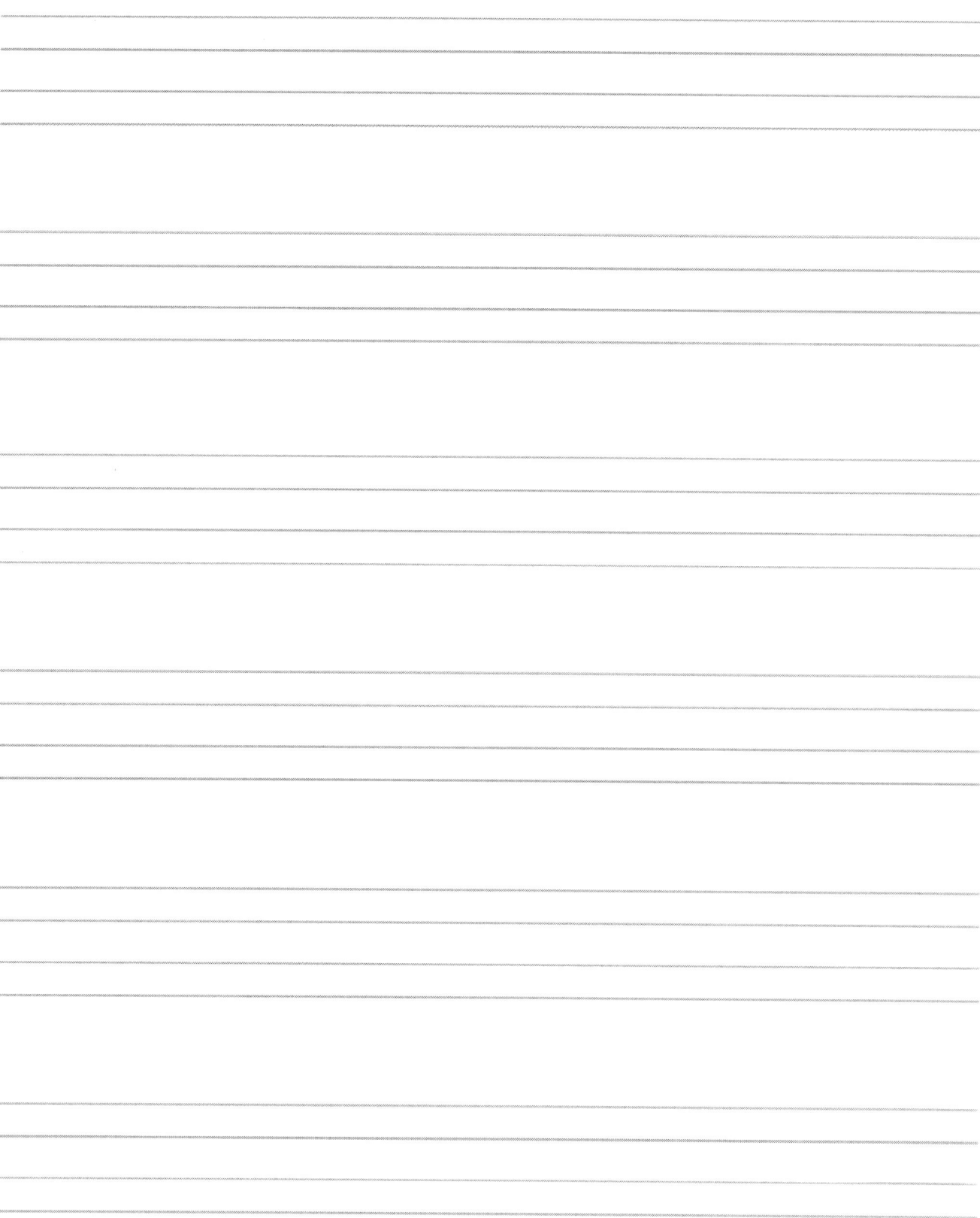

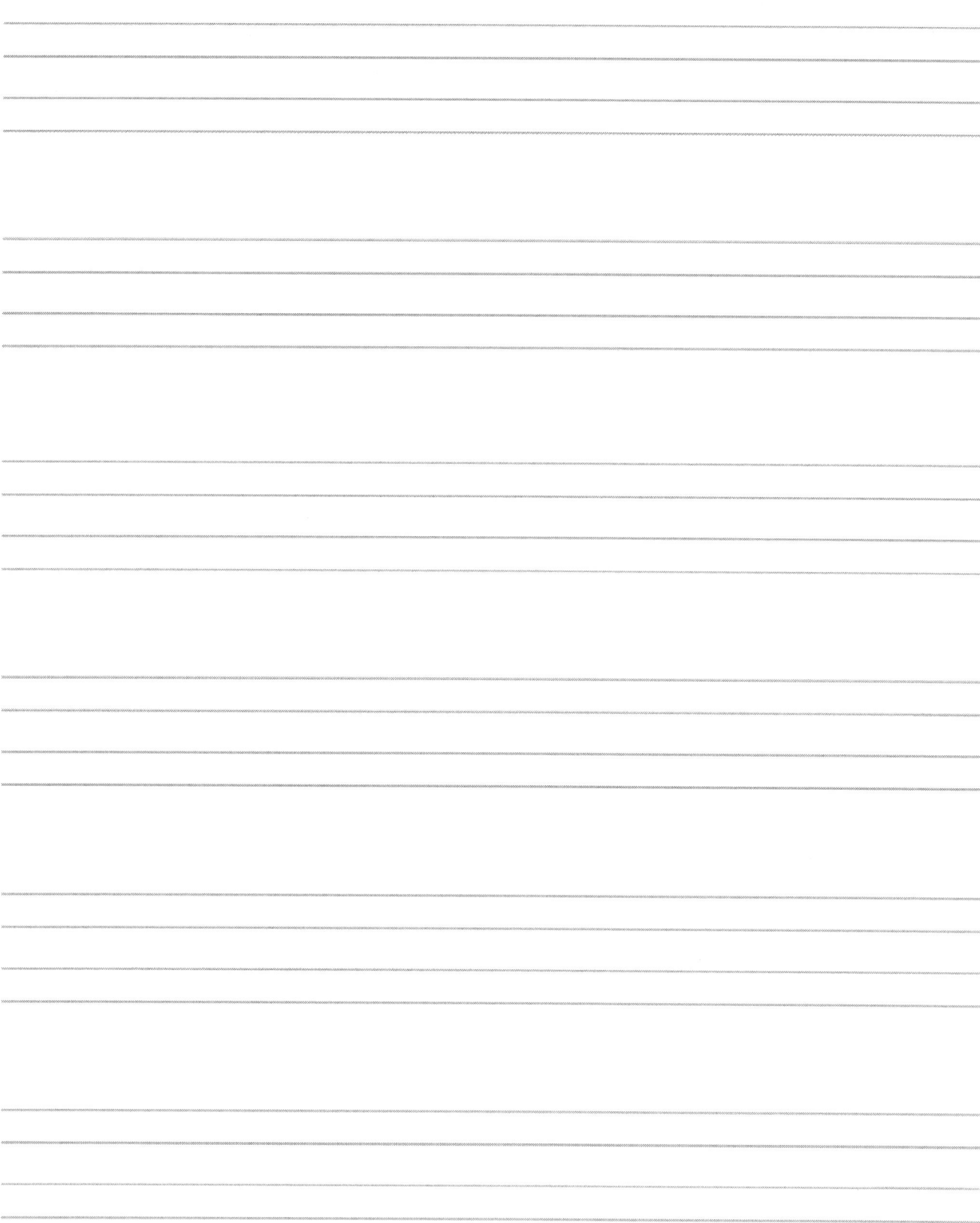

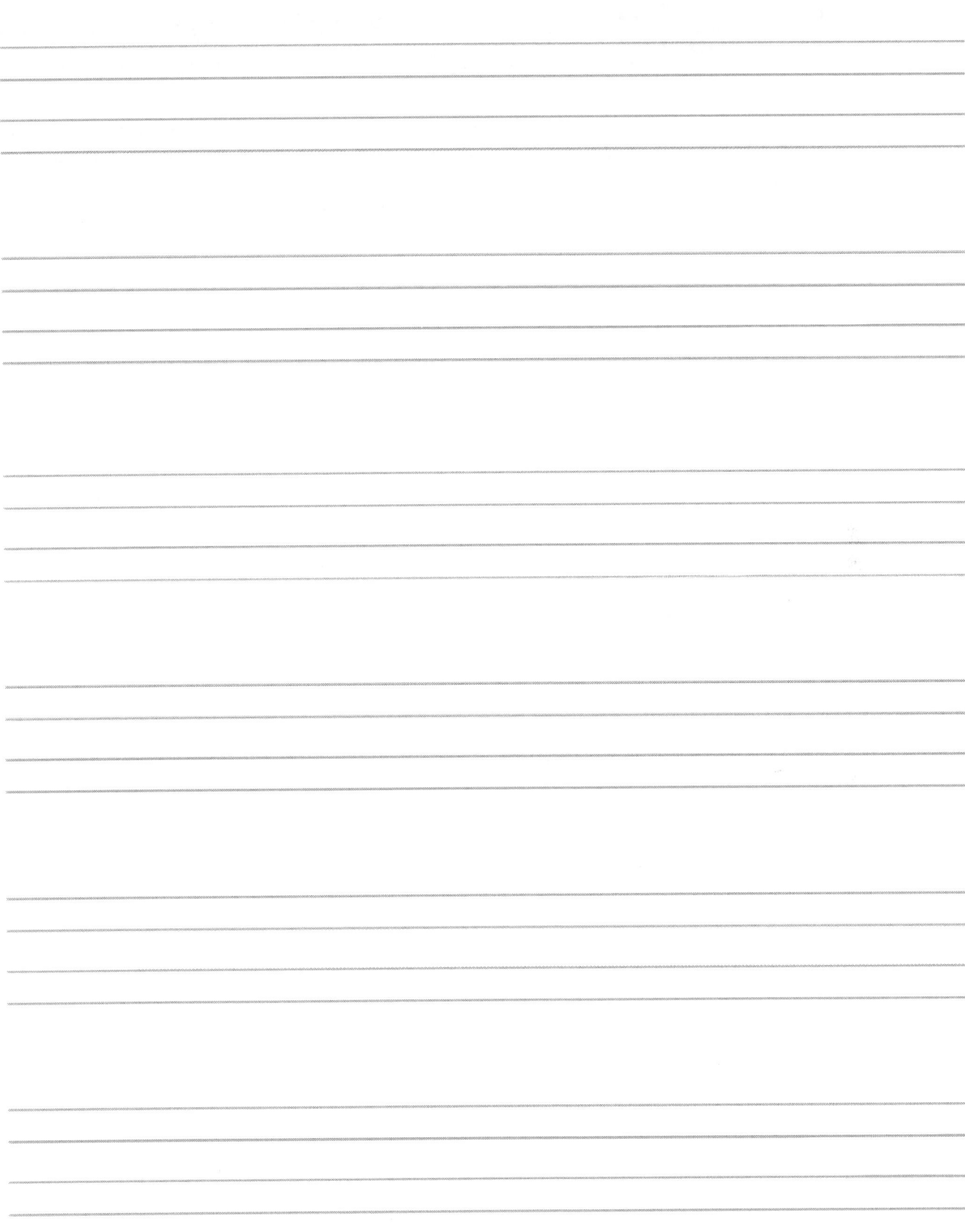

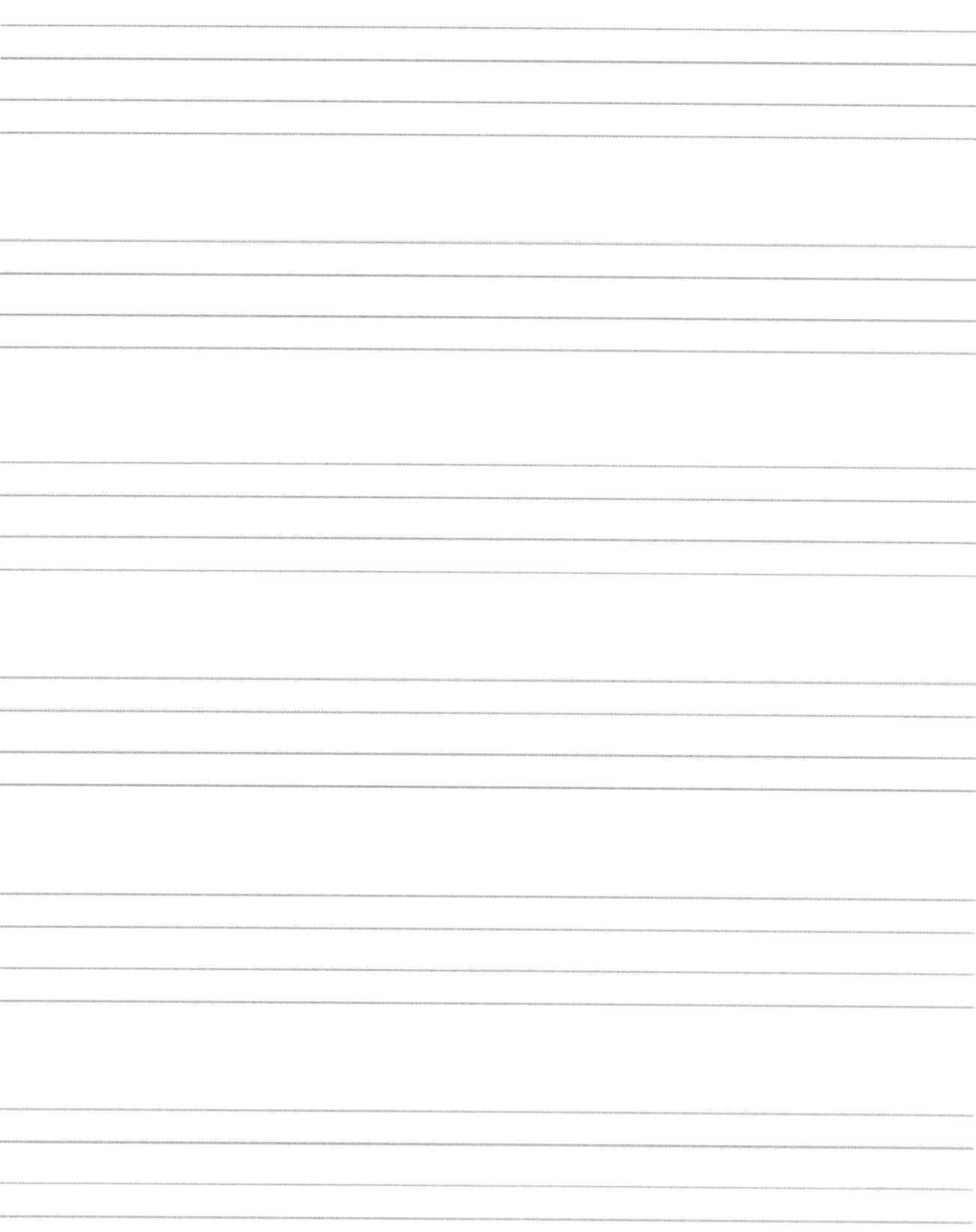

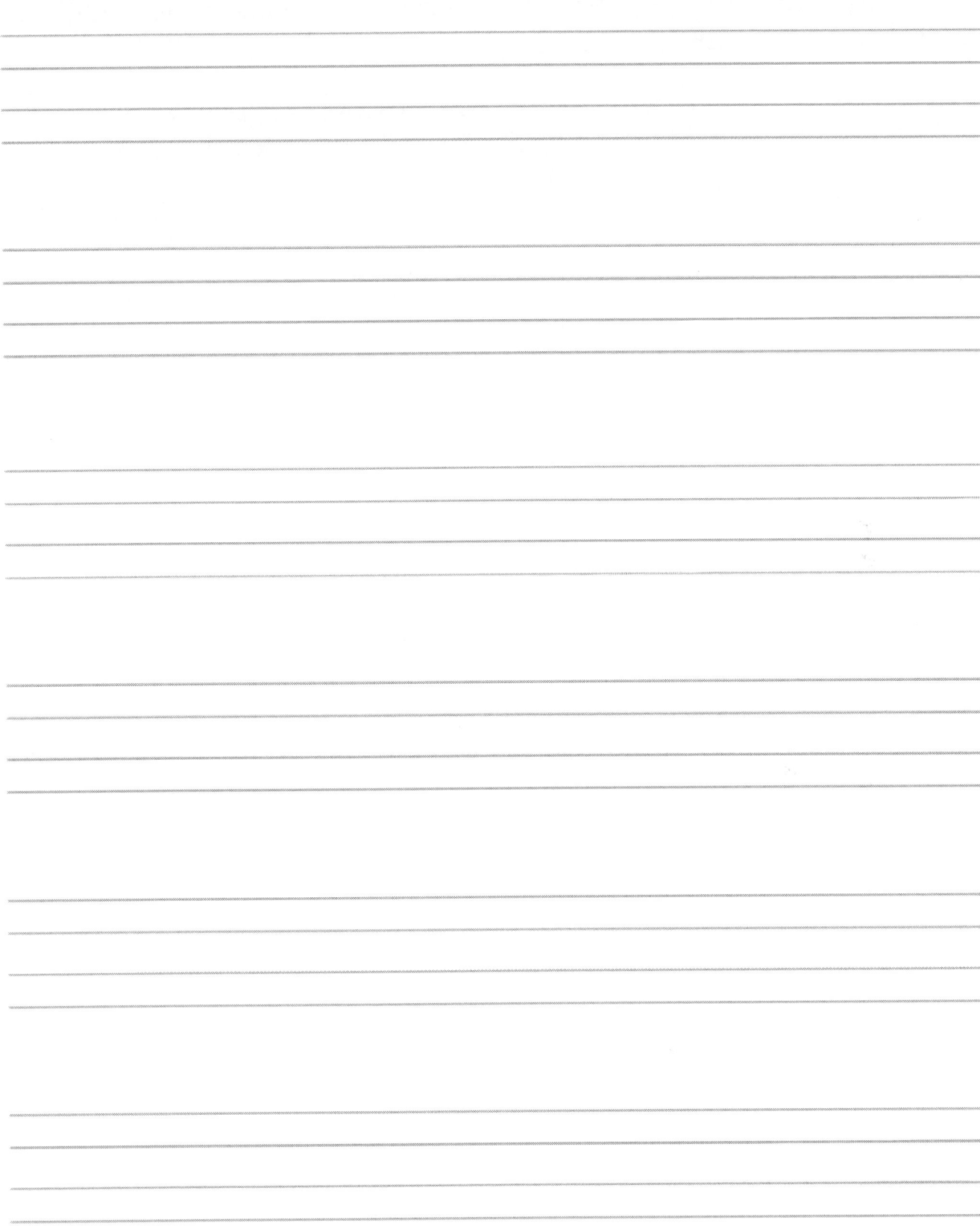

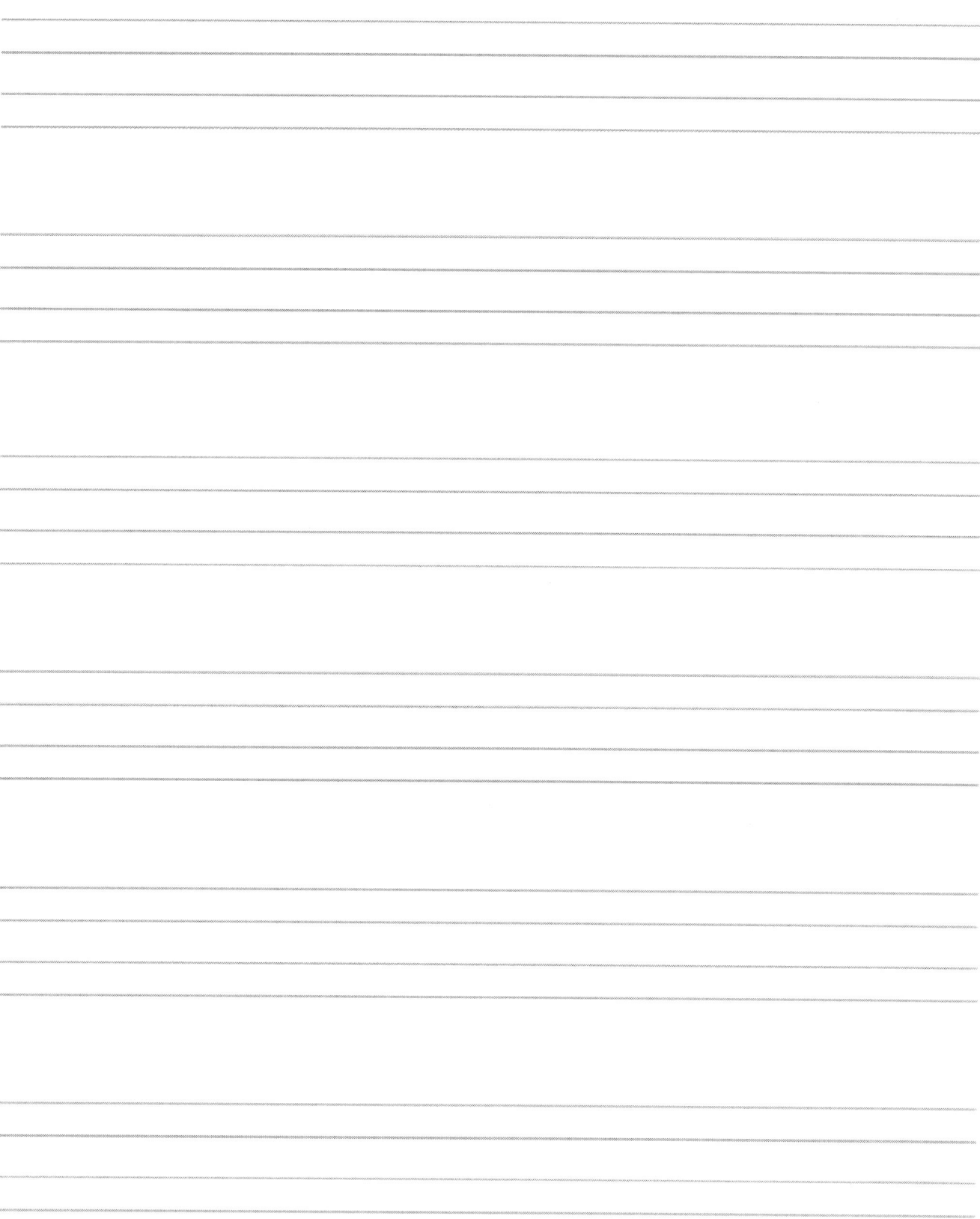

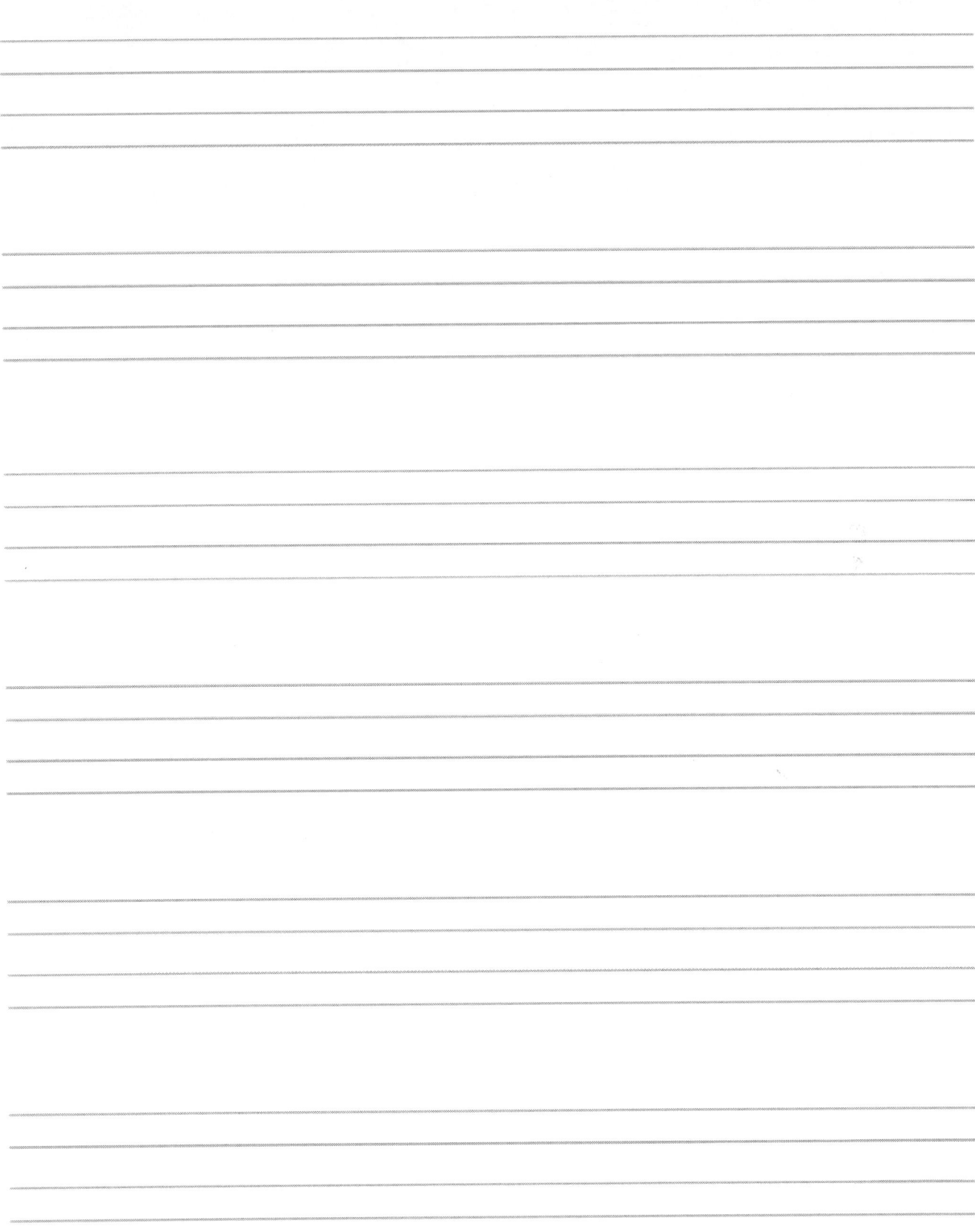

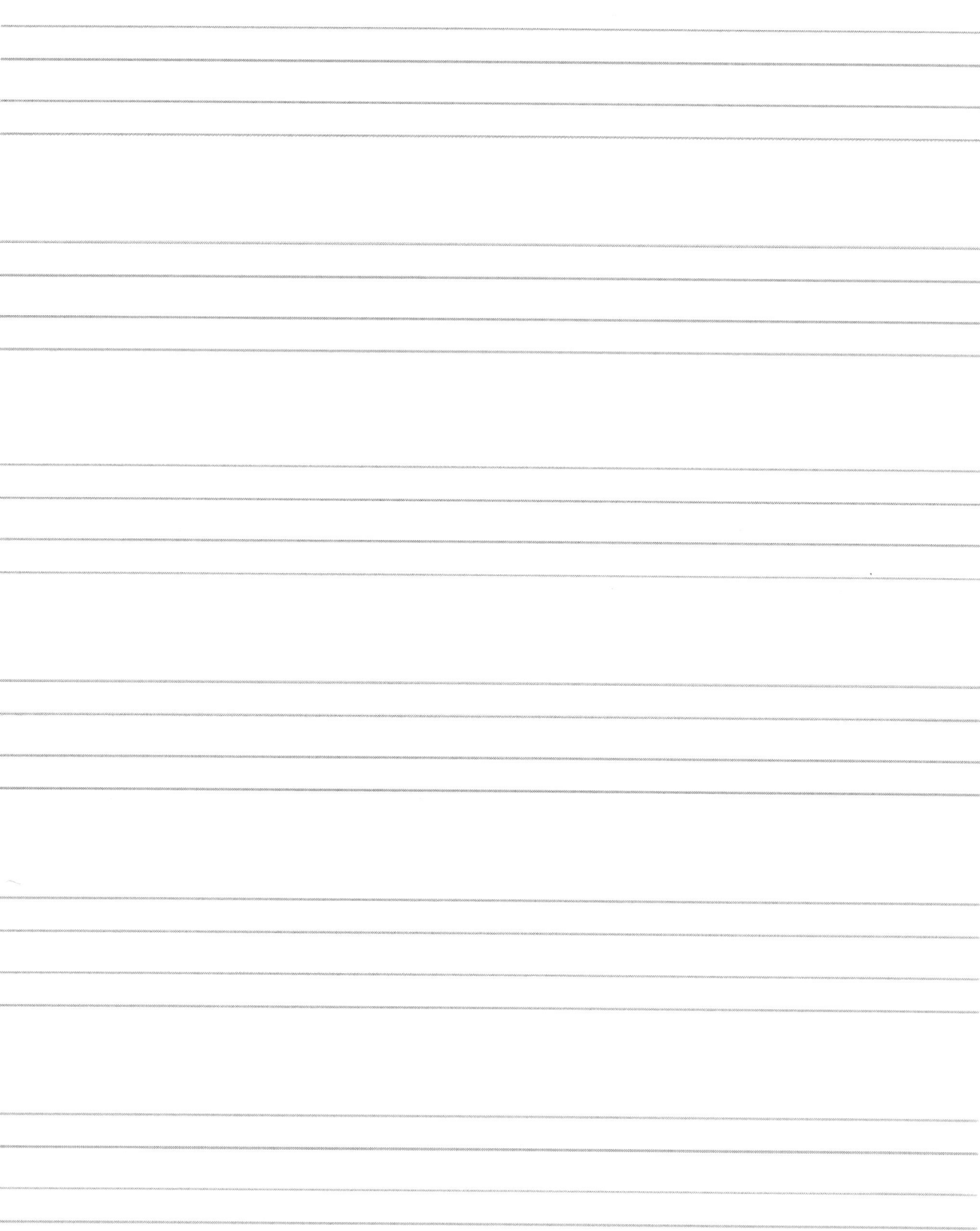

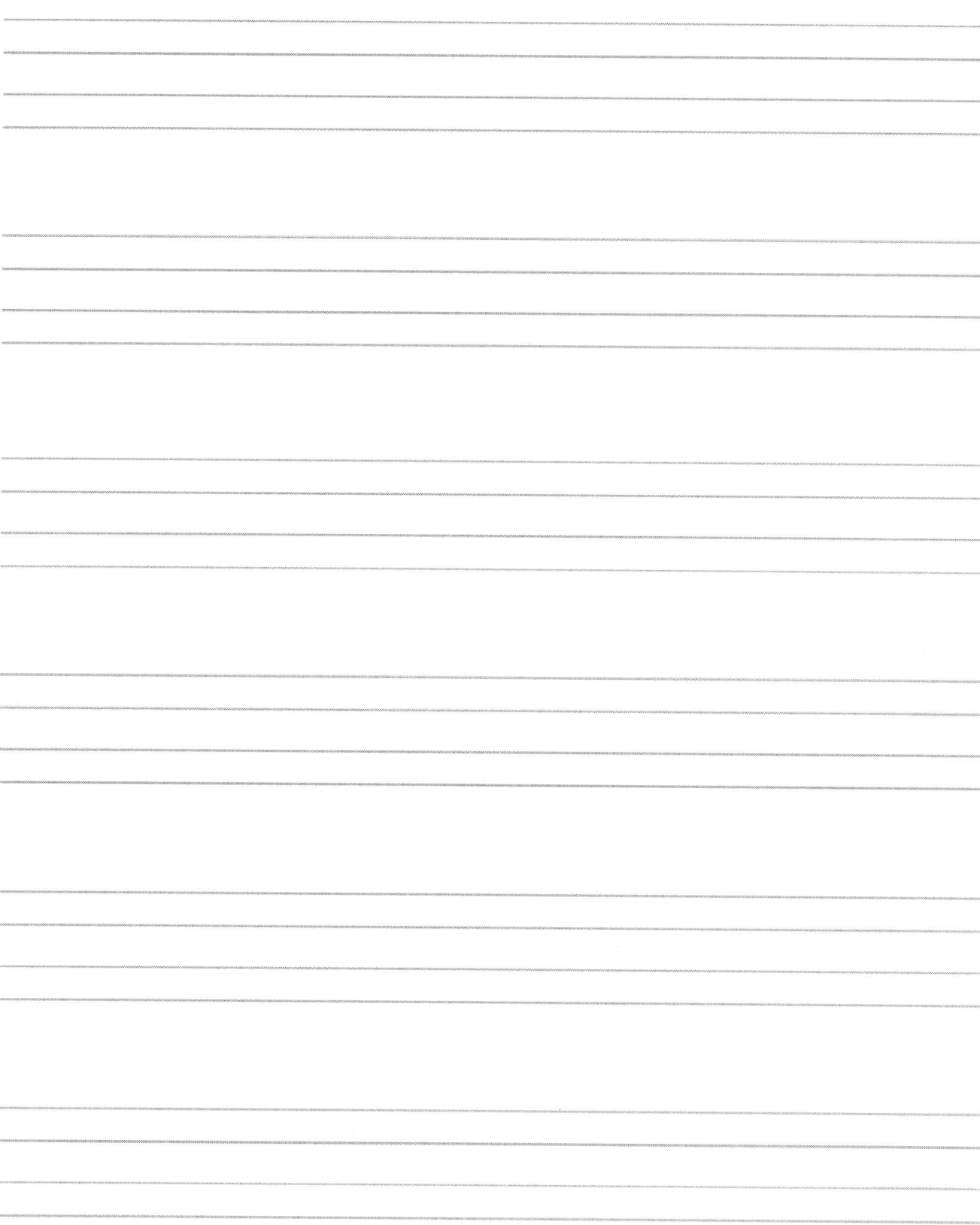

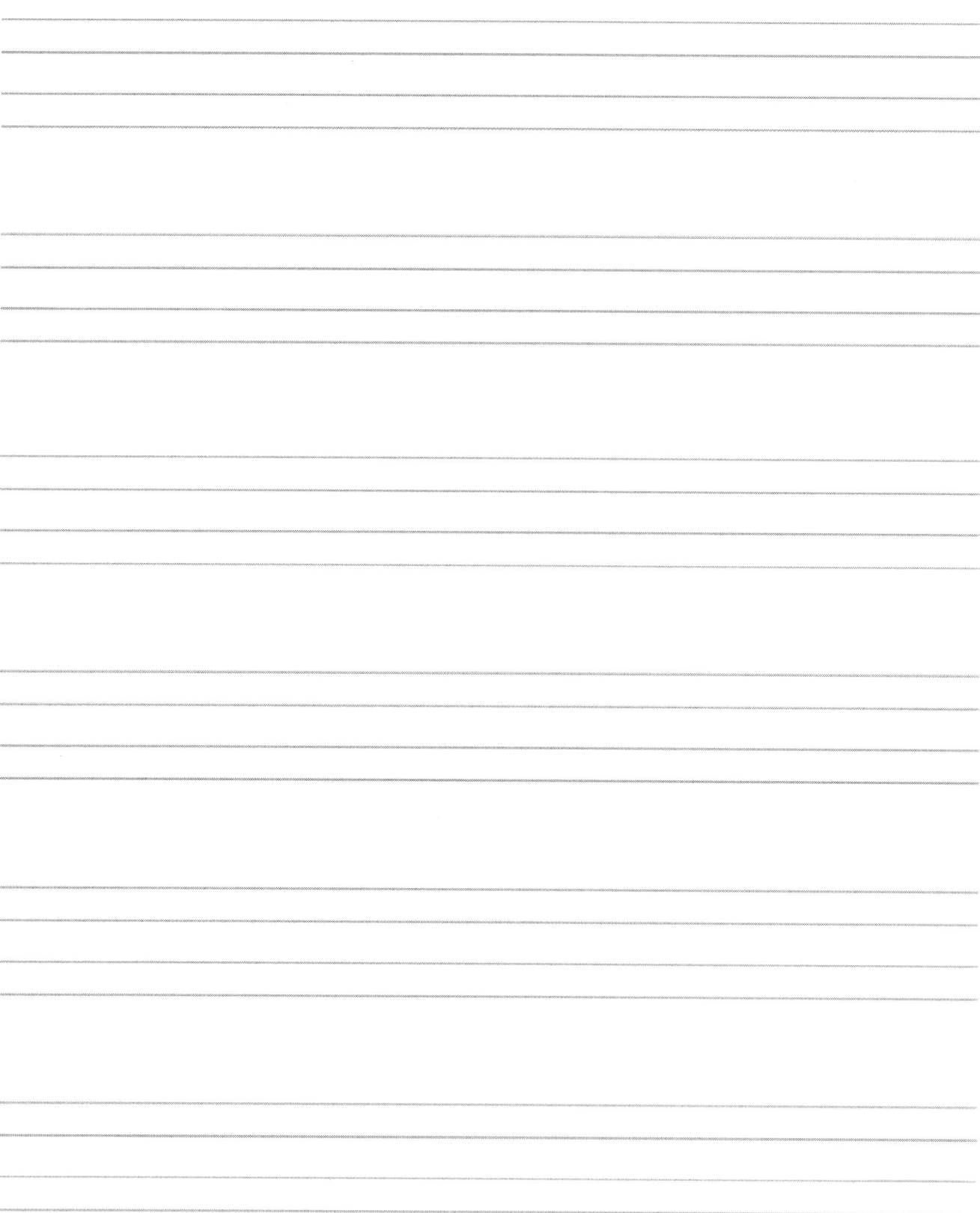

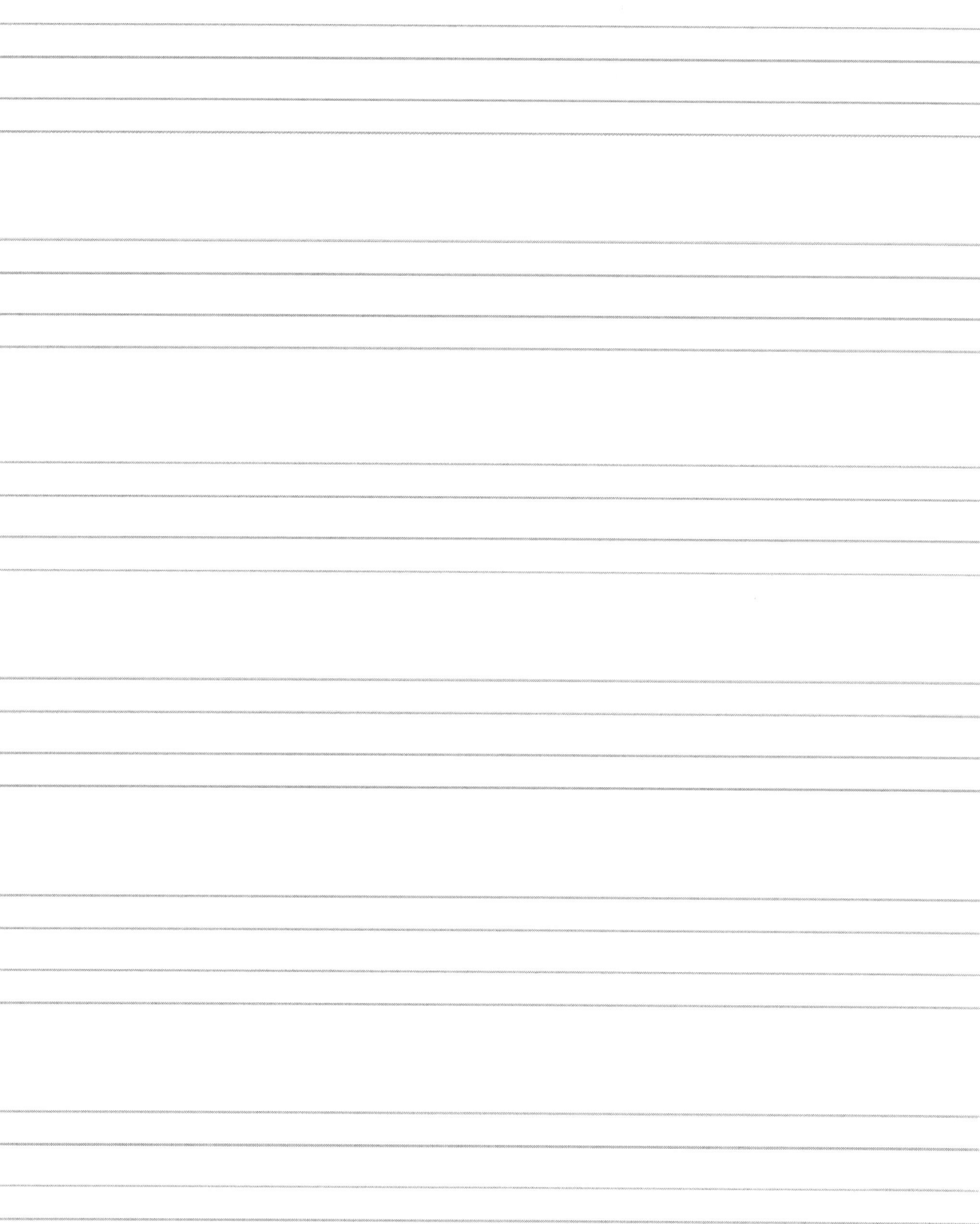

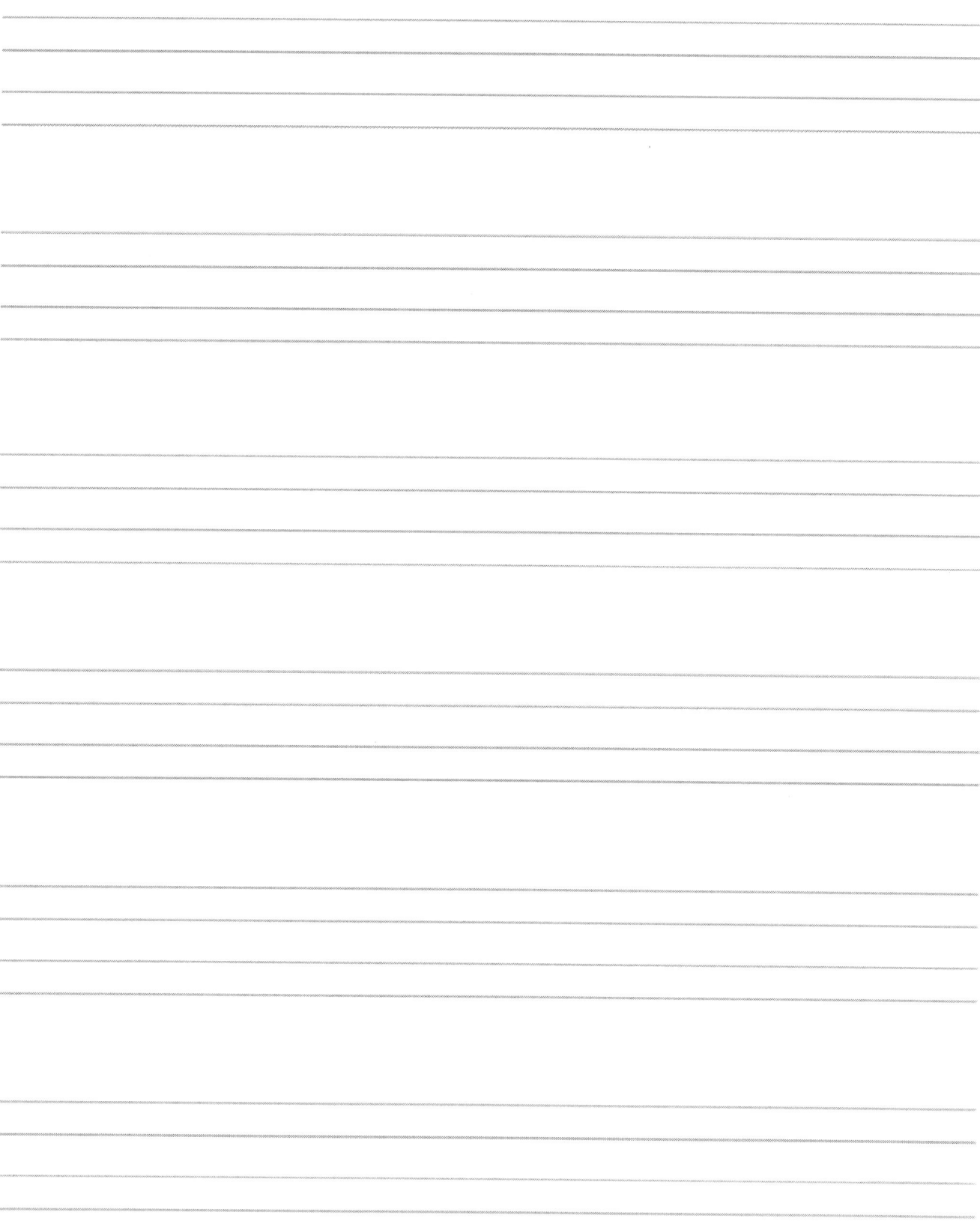

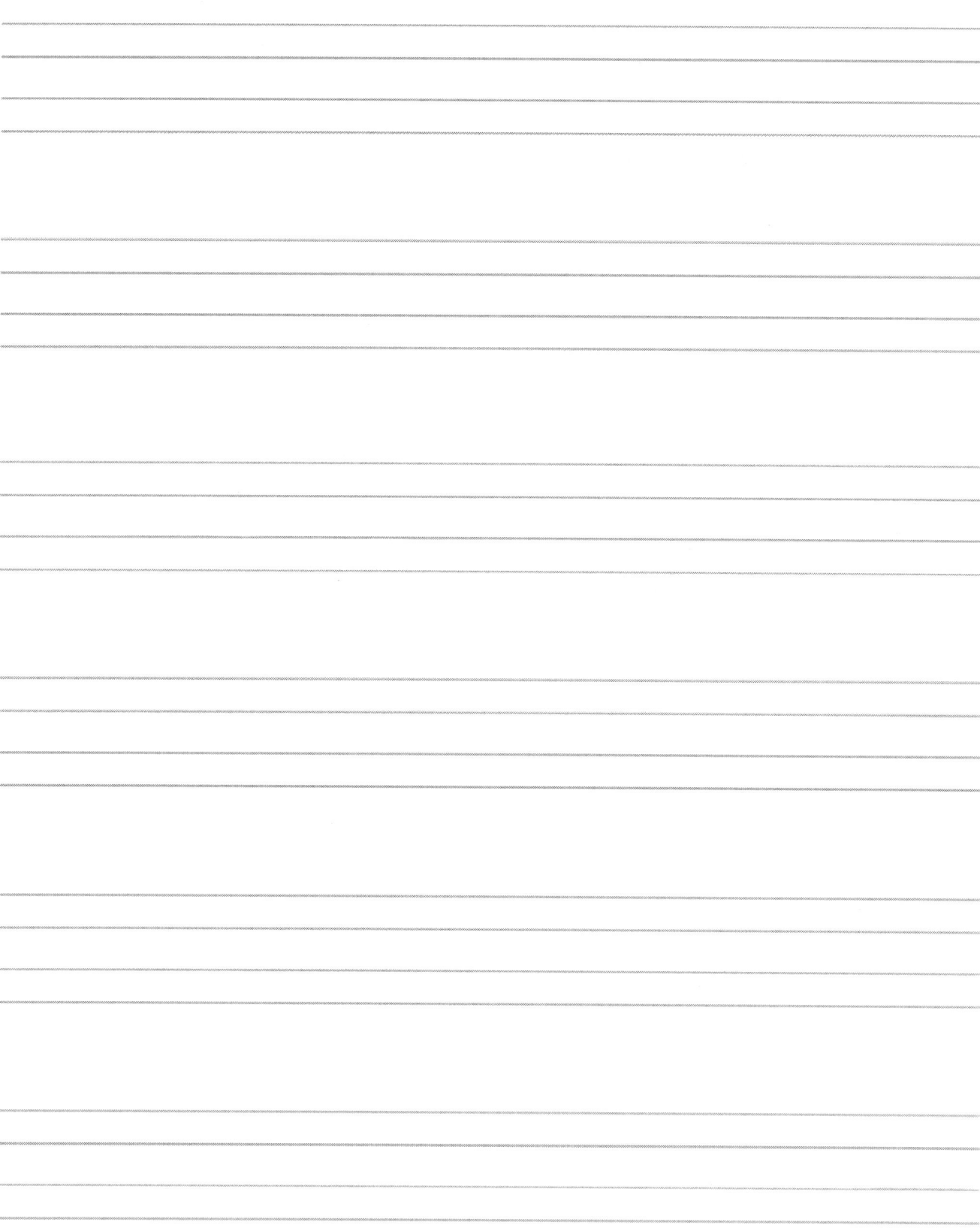

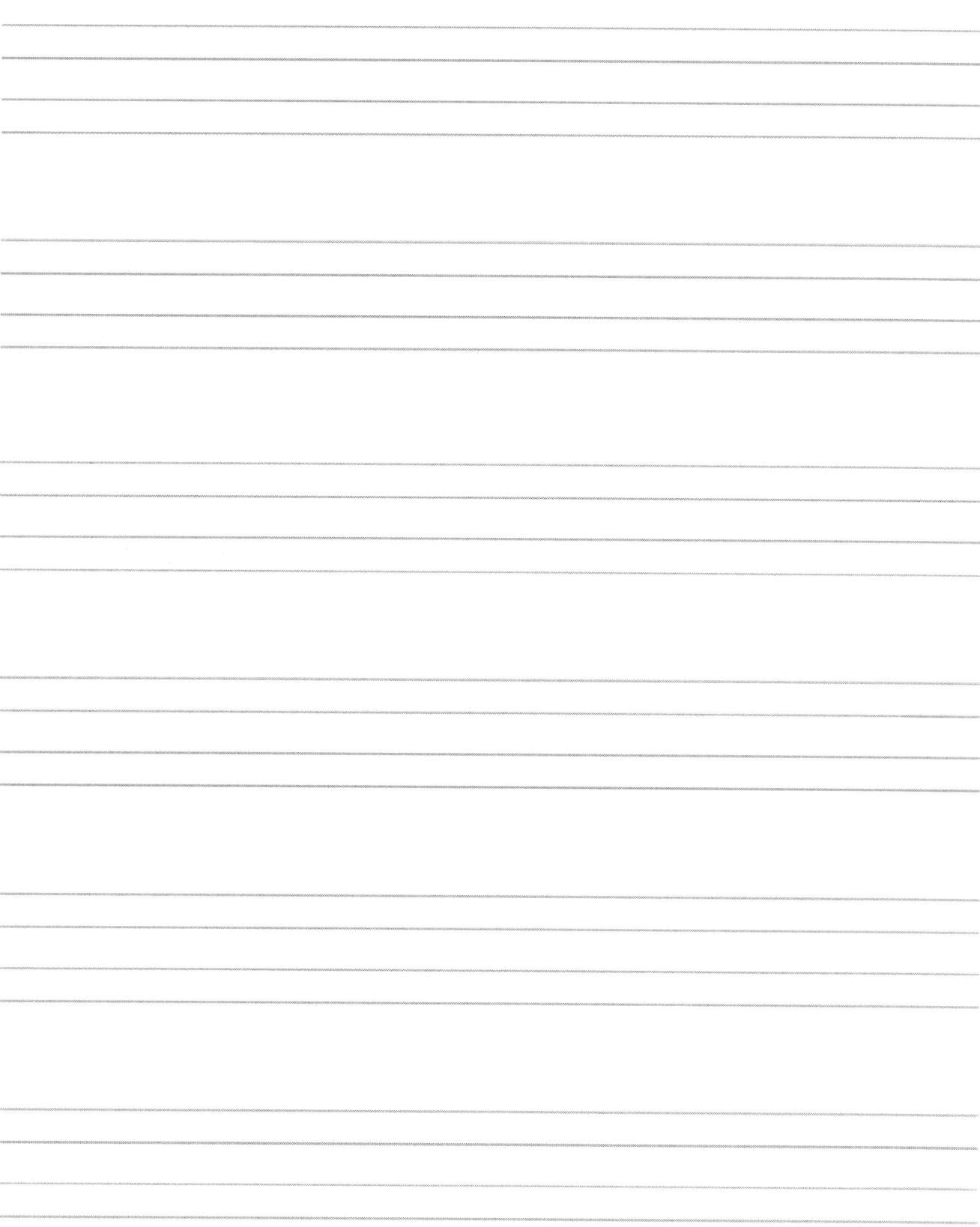

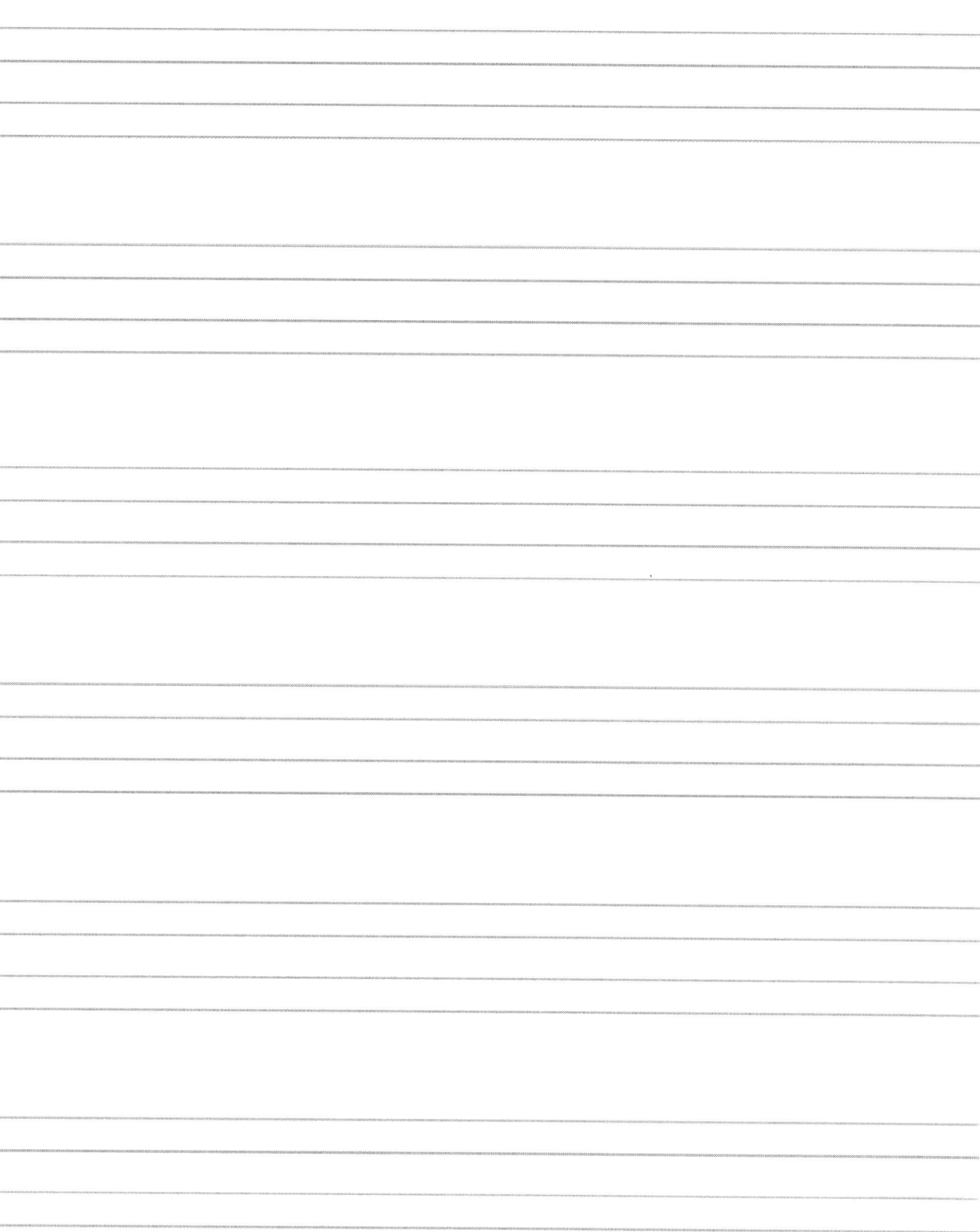

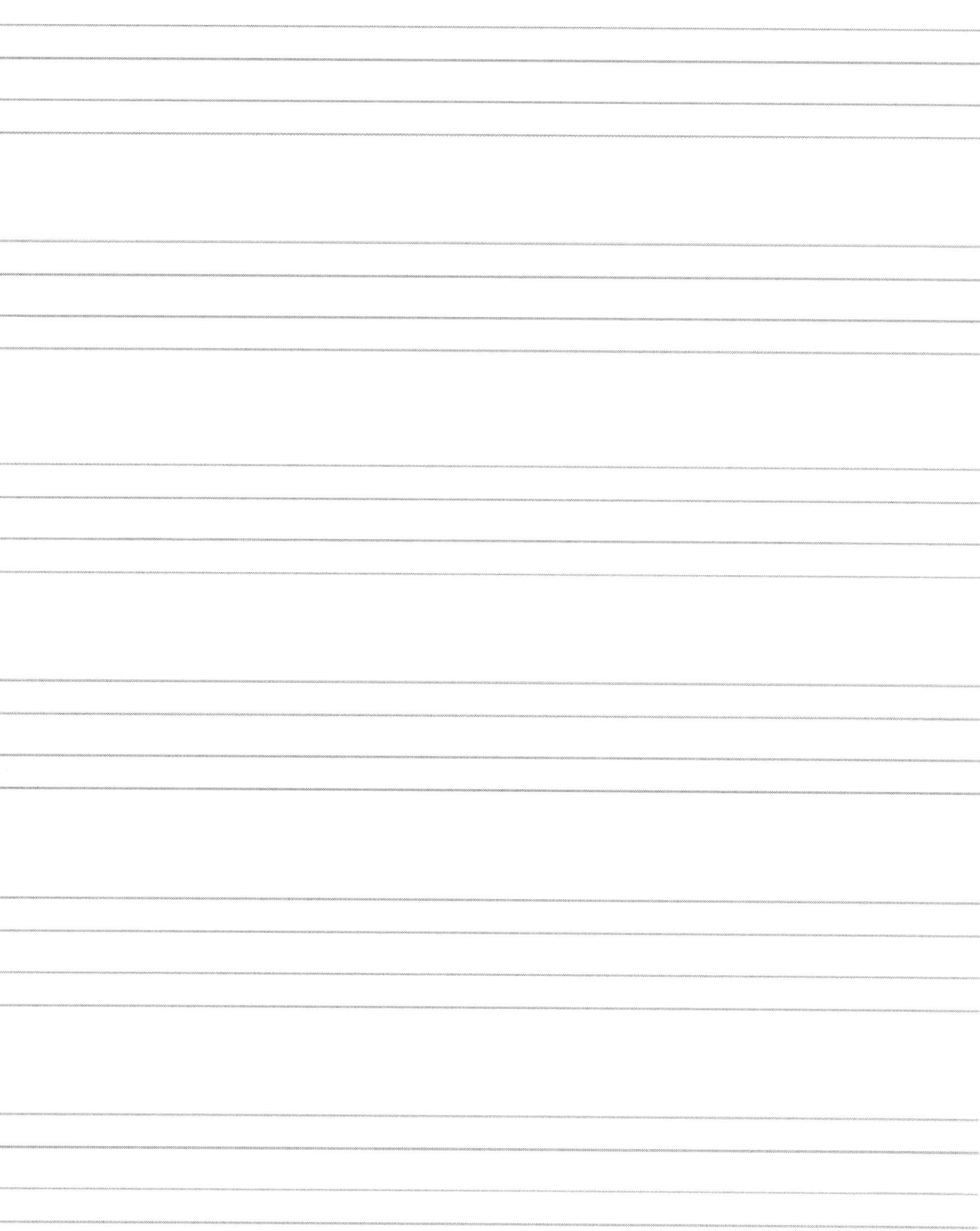

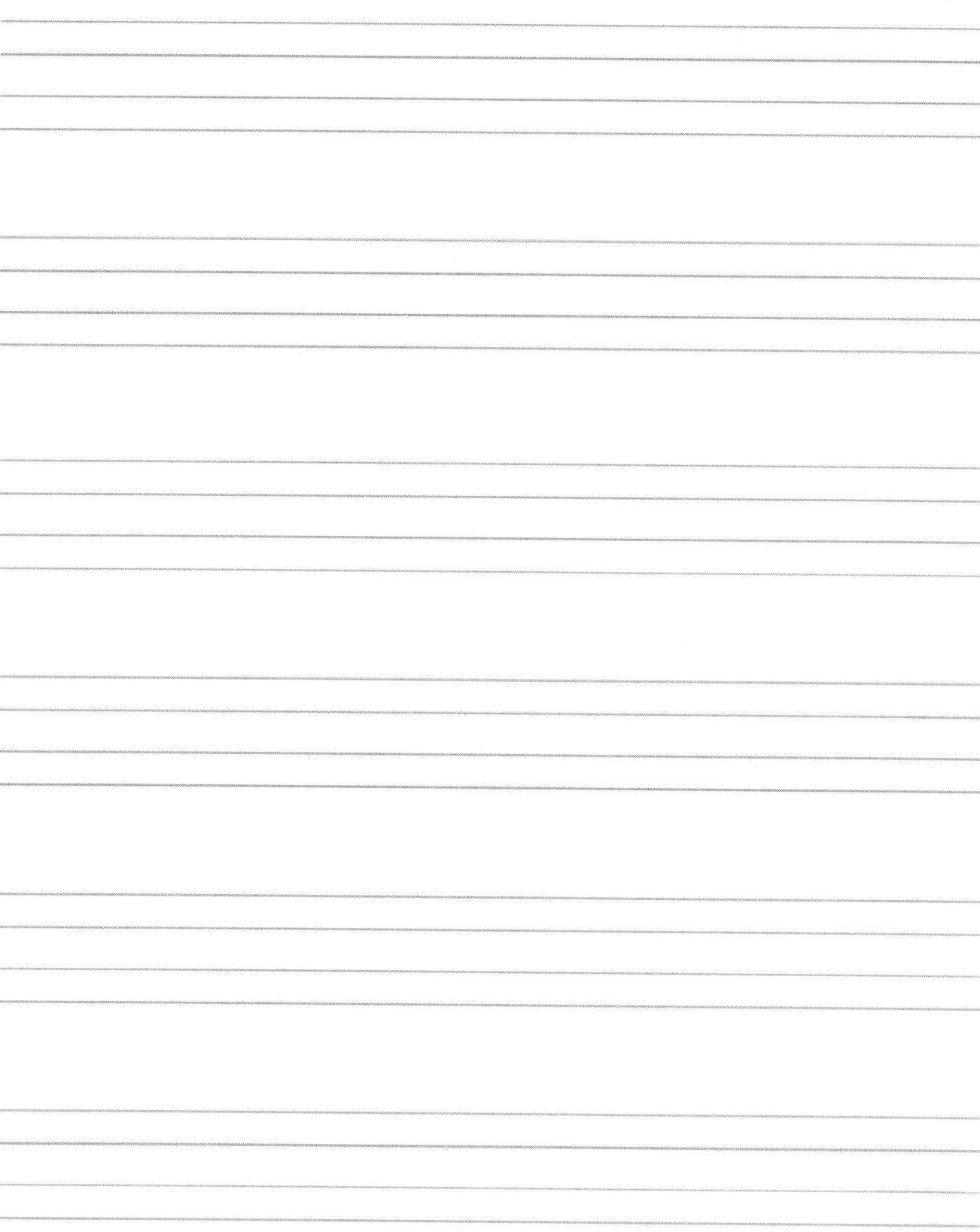

Paper 2

Paper 3

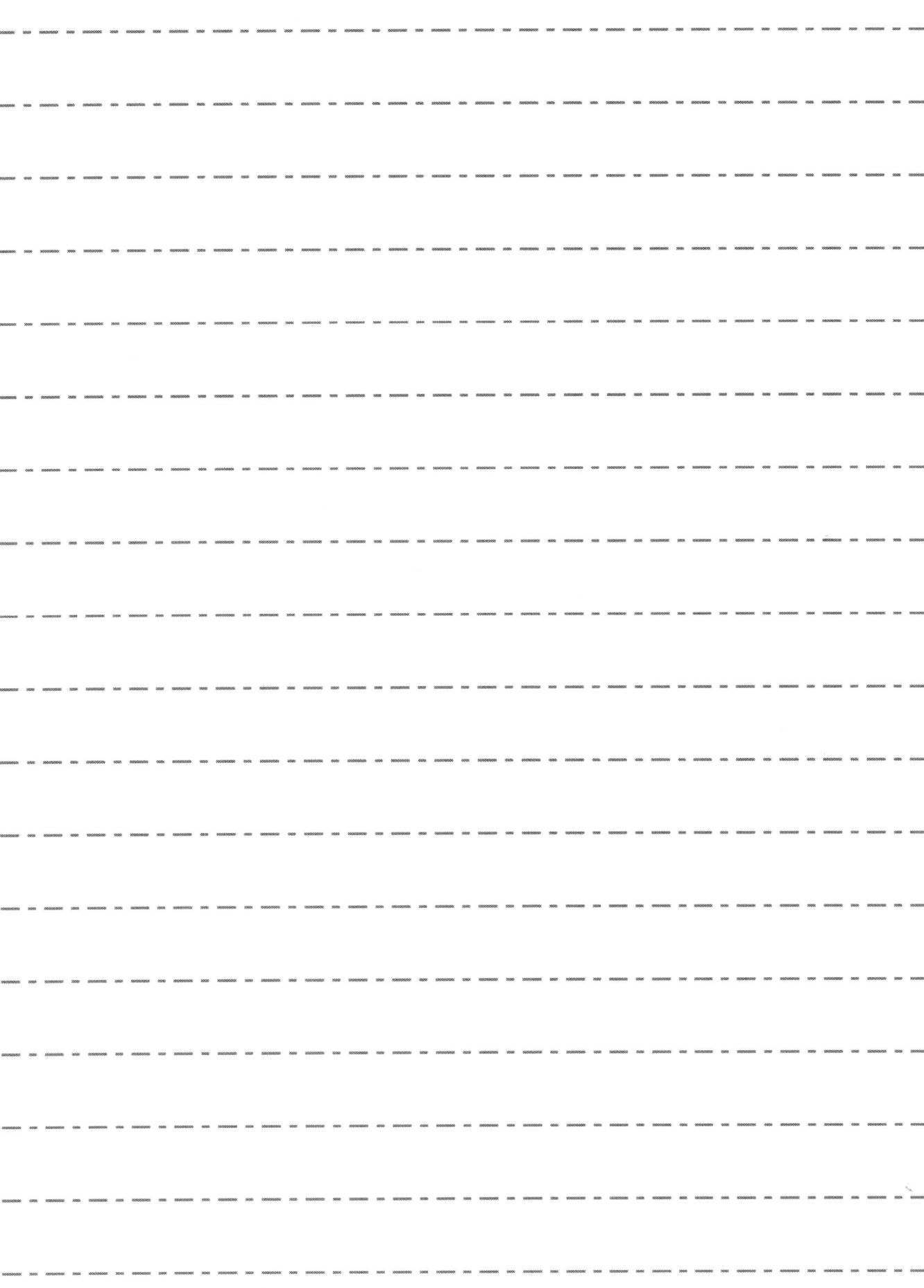

Paper 4

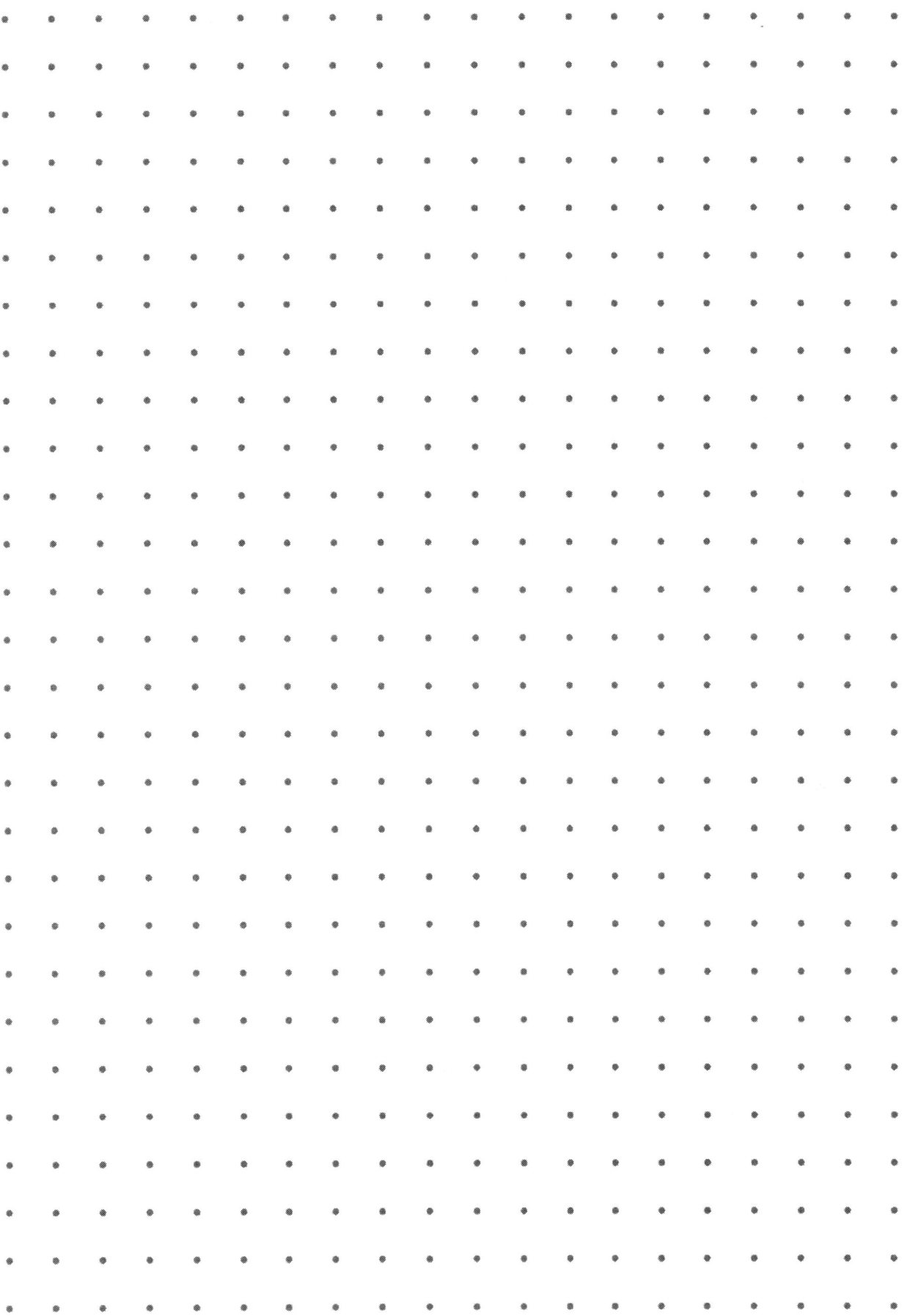

Made in the USA
Middletown, DE
26 May 2017